Mommy, What Time Is It?

WRITTEN BY:- TIMSHA R. BATISTE
ILLUSTRATED BY:- RESHMA MANSOORI

Copyright © 2021 by Timsha R. Batiste
All rights reserved. No part of this publication may be reproduced, distributed, or transmitted in any form or by any means, including photocopying, recording, or other electronic or mechanical methods, without the prior written permission of the publisher, except in the case of brief quotations embodied in critical reviews and certain other noncommercial uses permitted by copyright law. For permission requests, write to the author, addressed "Attention: Permissions" at info@batistestories.com.
Timsha R. Batiste
Houston, Texas
www.batistestories.com
Ordering Information:
For details, contact: info@batistestories.com
"Mommy, What Time Is It?"
Paperback- 978-1-7360761-6-3
eBook- 978-1-7360761-7-0
"Dominique's Healthy Choices"
Hardback ISBN- 978-1-7360761-4-9
Paperback ISBN- 978-1-7360761-3-2
Ebook ISBN- 978-1-7360761-5-6
My Hair Power"
Hardback ISBN: 978-1-7360761-0-1
EBook ISBN: 978-1-7360761-1-8
Paperback ISBN: 978-1-7360761-2-5
Available @ Amazon.com, Lulu, and Ingramsparks
Printed in the United States of America

Acknowledgement

I would like to thank God for allowing me to bring to life children's books.

I would like to thank my lovely husband Roy Batiste for encouraging me, always being supportive and for being a great father.

I would like to thank Ms.Shenna Bradley for being a listening ear on all my ideas. Ms.Shenna you are definitely a "Motivator".

I would like to thank my lovely daughter Serenity for inspiring me to be better. Serenity you have changed my life and I am so Blessed to have you.

A special thanks to my nieces and nephew Aniyah, Tiana, and Torrey. Thanks for being such an inspiration.

Cassandra Stallings you are my number one fan, thanks for always being there for me. You have always believed in me no matter what I do.

Dedication

Dear Serenity,

You're very special, never let anyone tell you otherwise. When you were born my life changed in a very special way. I wanted to become a better ME. I knew life with you would never be the same. God has blessed your mom with a gift, that gift is YOU! Serenity you're beautiful, unique, smart, remarkable, humorous, caring, loving and so much more. Therefore, I am so grateful to have you as my daughter. I want you to always remember to keep God first, no matter what. My prayer is that God be with you always.

Love you much,

Mommy

"Serenity, it's time to wake up!"

"Mommy, can I have five more minutes?"

"Okay, but then you have to get up and brush your teeth."

Serenity's mom checked her teeth. "Serenity, say cheese!"

"Cheese!" Serenity said as she smiled wide. "What time is it now, Mommy?"

"It's time to sing the morning song."

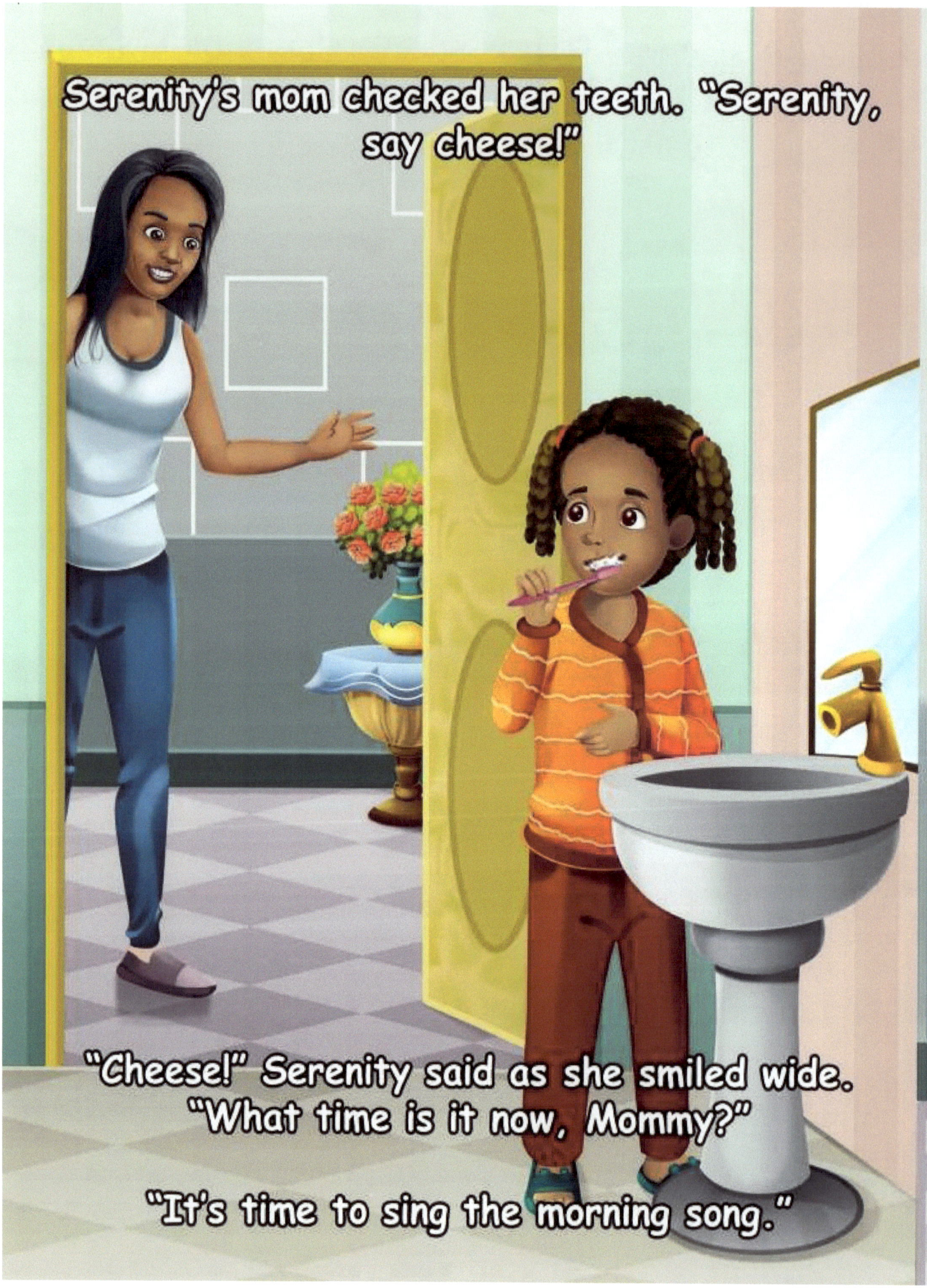

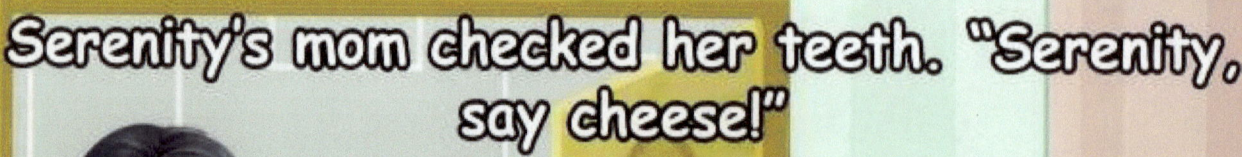

Serenity smiled. "What about Daddy?"

"Let's go find him and we'll sing to him," her mom said.

Serenity's dad was in the kitchen.

"Good morning, Daddy, we are fine. How are you?" Serenity sang.

"It's time for Daddy to leave," Serenity's mom said.

"Can I go to work with you, Daddy?"

"No, baby girl, you've got to stay here and keep Mommy company." Serenity and her mom kissed Daddy goodbye.

Serenity's mom lifted up each flash card as Serenity thought of animals.

"A is for Alligator or Ant.
B is for Bear or Bee.
C is for Camel or Cat.

D is for Dog or Dolphin, and E is for…" For a few seconds, Serenity couldn't think of anything, but then she said, "Eagle and also Elephant!"

"Great job!" her mom said. "Now it's time for another game. When you see the picture, give me its shape and color.

"Are you ready, Serenity?"

"Yes! There's a red triangle. The next one is a blue circle. The third one is a black octagon. The fourth one is a purple rectangle."

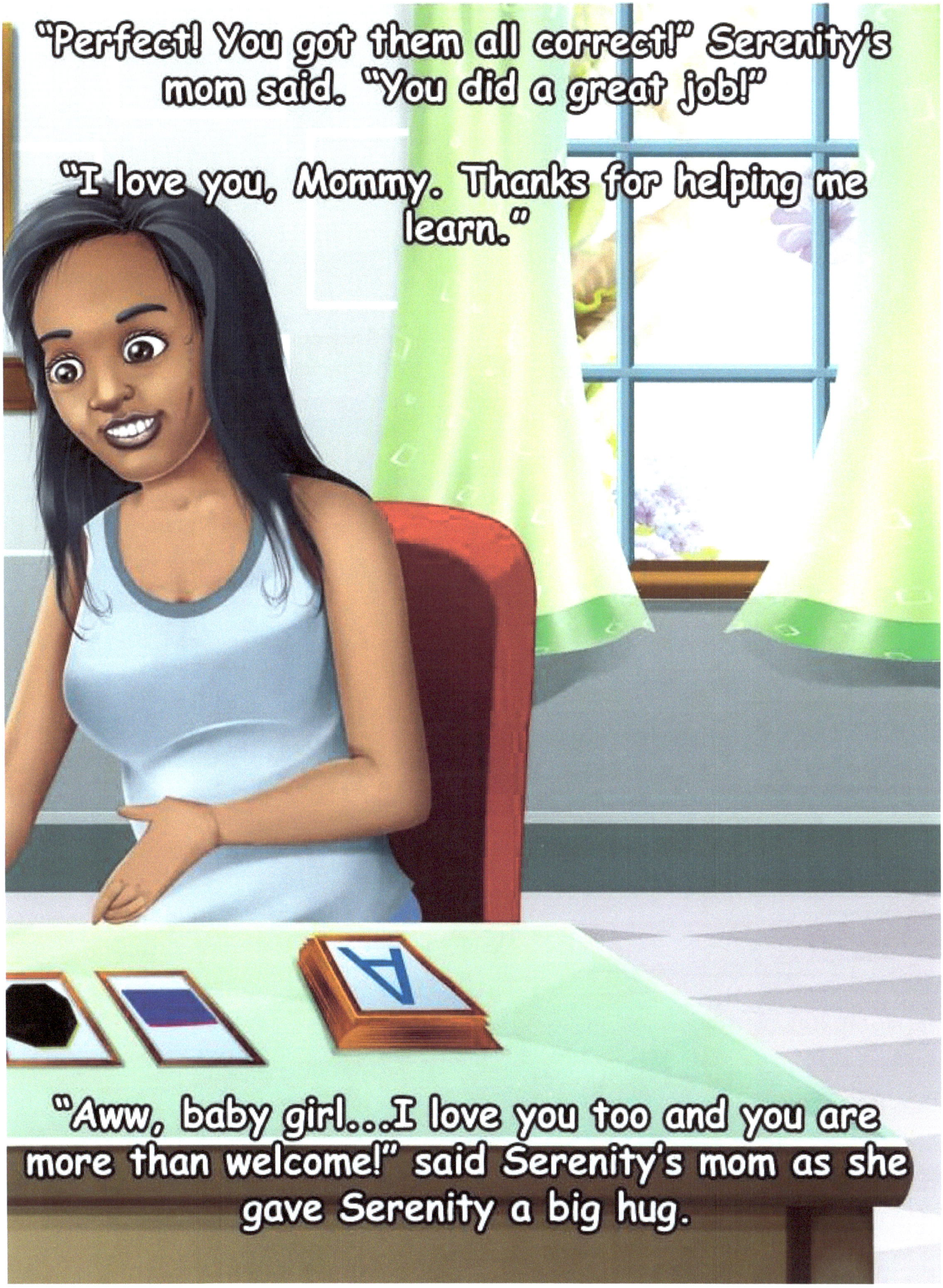

"Perfect! You got them all correct!" Serenity's mom said. "You did a great job!"

"I love you, Mommy. Thanks for helping me learn."

"Aww, baby girl...I love you too and you are more than welcome!" said Serenity's mom as she gave Serenity a big hug.

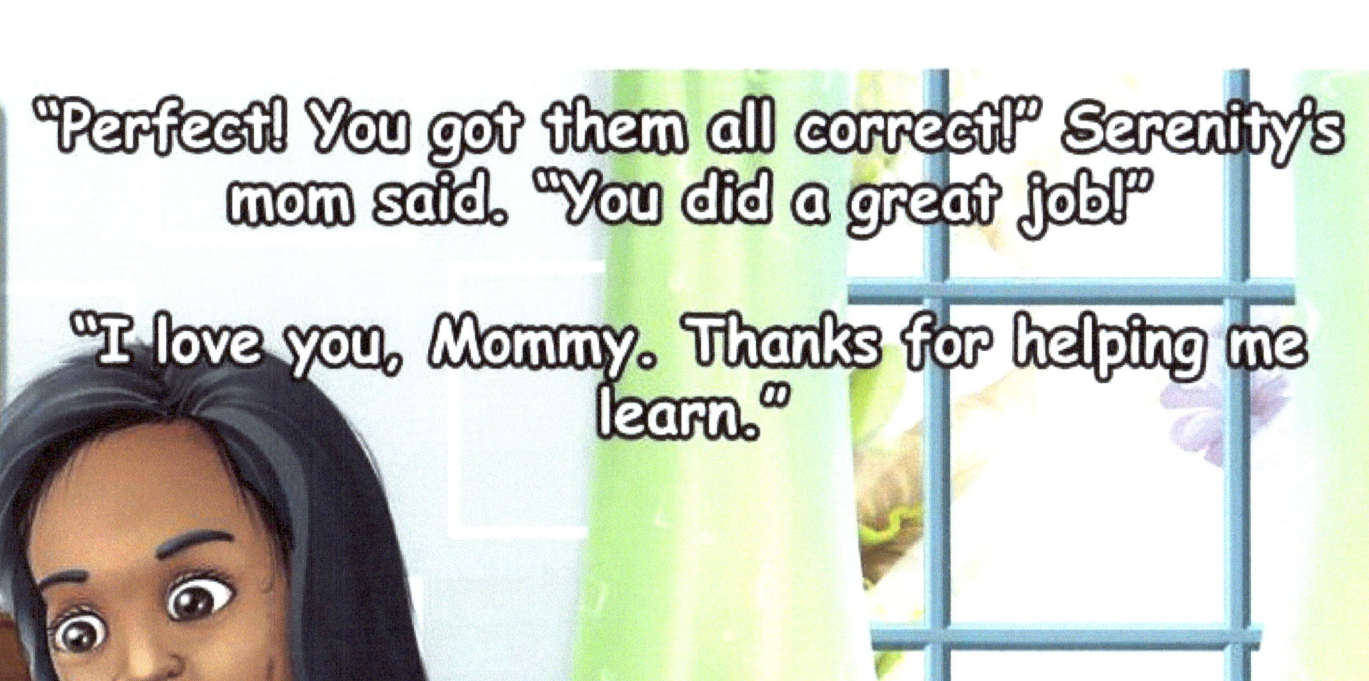

"Mommy, what time is it?"

"Time for your show."

"Mommy, dance with me!" Serenity ran into the living room. Her mom followed her.

"But where's the music?"

"It's okay. We don't need music, Mommy. We can dance without it." The two of them danced in circles and held hands.

Then, Serenity sat down to watch her show with the snack her mom had fixed.

After the show was over, Serenity asked "What time is it now?"

"It's lunchtime. Sit at the table. I'll fix your favorite lunch."

"Yay! My favorite is grilled cheese with fruit and chocolate milk. Yummy!"

"If you eat everything and make a happy, empty plate we'll do something fun later."

"My plate's happy, Mommy. What time is it now?"

"It's time for a nap."

Serenity picked one of her favorite dolls to nap with. Her mom sang Twinkle, Twinkle Little Star to her and Serenity fell asleep. Her mom took a nap too.

When her mom woke up, she gently woke Serenity up.

"What time is it now, Mommy?" Serenity said sleepily.

"It's time to go to the park!"

"Yay! Can I ride my bike and take my bubbles!"

"Yes, you can. You've been a good girl today!"

Serenity put shorts on under her dress and they got her bike. The park was not far away so she jumped on and started to ride.
"Mommy! You can't catch me!"

"Yes, I can! What are you doing?" her mom asked.

"I'm making a circle with my bike!" Serenity called out as she giggled.

"Be careful. Don't fall," her mom said. When they got to the park, Serenity got off her bike and ran to the swings.

"Please push me, Mommy!" Serenity said with a cute smile.

"Okay. Here we go!"

As her mom pushed her higher and higher, Serenity laughed as if her daddy were tickling her.

After that, Serenity was tired. "Is it time to go home now?"

"Yes," said her mom. "Hold my hand and we'll walk home with your bike."

"Thank you for taking me to the park and having fun with me."

"Ohhhhh... you're very welcome, baby!"

"I'm ready for bed. What time is it now?" But her mom didn't have to tell her because she heard the garage door opening. "It's time for Daddy to come home!"

"I'll help you find a hiding spot so you can scare Daddy. Then, I'll go cook dinner. How about the closet?"

Serenity nodded and hid. When her Daddy opened the front door, she jumped out and yelled "Raaaaaa!"

When Serenity's mom finished cooking, she put dinner on the table. Serenity, Mommy, and Daddy enjoyed eating their dinner together.

While they ate, Serenity shared everything that happened with her daddy.

"Wow! That was a full day. Are you tired, Serenity?"

"Yes, Daddy. I'm kind of tired. Mommy, what time is it?"

"What do you think, Serenity?" her mom asked.

"I think it might be bedtime."

"Yes," her mom said. "But first you have to brush your teeth."

"Mommy, can you tell me the story about when I was a little baby?"

"Sure, baby doll. Let's crawl into bed together and I'll tell you all about that very special time."

www.ingramcontent.com/pod-product-compliance
Lightning Source LLC
LaVergne TN
LVHW072058070426
835508LV00002B/150